Helping Out

At the Farm

Judith Heneghan

WAYLAND

First published in 2011 by Wayland

Copyright © Wayland 2011

Wayland
Hachette Children's Books
338 Euston Road
London NW1 3BH

Wayland Australia
Level 17/207 Kent Street
Sydney, NSW 2000

Editor: Louise John
Designer: Robert Walster, Big Blu Design

British Library Cataloguing in Publication Data

Anderson, Judith, 1965-
  At the dairy farm. -- (Helping out)
  1. Dairy farms--Juvenile literature. 2. Dairy cattle--
  Juvenile literature. 3. Dairy farmers--Juvenile
  literature.
  I. Title II. Series
  636.2'142-dc22

ISBN-13: 9780750264884

Printed in China
Wayland is a division of Hachette Children's Books,
an Hachette UK company. www.hachette.co.uk

Picture acknowledgements
All photography by Andy Crawford

With thanks to Peter Shaw at Bishop's Farm, Swindon.

Contents

An early start

Emily is spending the day at her neighbour's dairy farm. She's going to help Peter, the farmer, who starts work every day at 5am. Peter looks after 300 cows so there's plenty to do.

Each cow has its own stall, with plenty of straw to lie on.

First, Peter and Emily go to the cow barn to check that all the cows are well. Then Peter moves them to the yard outside. Now they can get some exercise.

These black and white cows are called Holsteins.

EMILY'S DIARY

It was hard getting out of bed so early. I felt better when we went to see the cows. It was warm in the barn, but very smelly!

Cleaning the cow barn

When the cows are outside, Peter and Emily clean out the stalls. First they clear away the dirty straw. Then they scrape out the **manure** and wash the floor with a hose.

Cleaning the stalls is a messy job.

That's
AMAZING!

Each cow produces
about 45 kg of manure
every day. That's
enough to fill six or
seven buckets!

Manure is the waste from a cow. It is very good for growing things. Peter grows crops such as **maize**, which he feeds to the cows in the winter.

Peter stores the manure in a big pit, before he spreads it on his fields.

Milking time

At 6am the cows are ready to be milked. Peter's **milking parlour** only has room for 28 cows so the other cows must wait their turn outside.

It takes about two hours for all the cows to be milked.

The cows are milked by machine. The machine gently squeezes the milk out of their **udders**. It doesn't hurt the cows. They stand quietly and eat some special food called '**cow cake**'. This helps them produce lots of good quality milk.

That's AMAZING!

In the past, people milked cows by hand. Each cow took about 20 minutes. It only takes five minutes by machine.

Peter attaches the machine to the cow's udders.

Feeding the calves

Most cows have a baby calf each year. When the calf is born, it drinks milk from its mother for a few days. Then it starts to drink milk from a bucket. The mother will carry on producing milk until the farmer chooses to stop milking her.

Emily helps to feed the new calves.

EMILY'S DIARY

Feeding the new calves was brilliant! They were very excited and they didn't mind me stroking them. This one is my favourite. Her name is Emily, too!

Emily notices that each calf or cow has tags in its ears. Peter explains that these tags are marked with each cow's identification number. They help him keep track of all his animals.

200637

Each calf is tagged soon after it is born.

Cleaning the equipment

After milking, Peter cleans all the **equipment**. He must make sure there is no old milk left in the pipes. This is very important. Old milk and dirty equipment can cause germs to spread.

Peter is cleaning the equipment.

The milk needs to be stored at a low temperature of less than 40 degrees.

The milk is stored in a big tank until a lorry comes to collect it. The tank keeps the milk cool and fresh.

That's AMAZING!

Milk isn't just for drinking. It is used to make dairy foods like cheese, butter, yoghurt and ice cream.
The milk from Peter's cows is used to make milk chocolate!

Feeding the cows

At last, Peter and Emily can go indoors to have their breakfast. Then it is time to give the cows their main meal of the day.

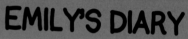

Emily and Peter make sure the cows have lots of fresh water to drink.

In the summer, the cows go out into the fields and eat fresh grass. They need to eat at least 50 kg of it each day. In winter there isn't enough fresh grass, so they eat the silage that Peter has stored.

The cow's meal is a special mix of soya, grain and fermented grass called **silage**.

15

Chewing the cud

After eating, the cows stand or lie down in their stalls and start to **digest** their food.

This cow is still chewing food that she ate a few hours ago.

That's AMAZING!

A cow has special muscles in its stomach to help it bring half-eaten food back up to its mouth. It's a bit like burping!

Cows don't eat like we do. They swallow food whole and it sits in their stomach until they are ready to bring it back up and chew on it some more. This helps them break down all that tough grass and silage. It is called 'chewing the cud'.

Fresh straw makes a comfortable bed for the cows.

A visit from the vet

At two o'clock the vet arrives at the farm. She has come to do a small operation on one of the cows. Emily talks quietly to the cow to help it stay calm. Then she helps the vet to give the cow an **injection**.

Peter uses a rope to get the cow to lie down. It does not hurt her.

Emily helps the vet to give the cow an injection.

Peter shows Emily how to change the cow's records on his computer. She adds the information about the operation and the injection, so that Peter can keep his records up to date.

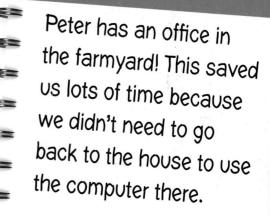

EMILY'S DIARY

Peter has an office in the farmyard! This saved us lots of time because we didn't need to go back to the house to use the computer there.

More milking

By the middle of the afternoon it is time to milk the cows again. If they aren't milked at least twice each day their udders become very uncomfortable.

Emily washes each cow's teats to stop them getting infected.

That's AMAZING!

Each dairy cow produces around 22 litres of milk a day. That's enough to fill 100 glasses!

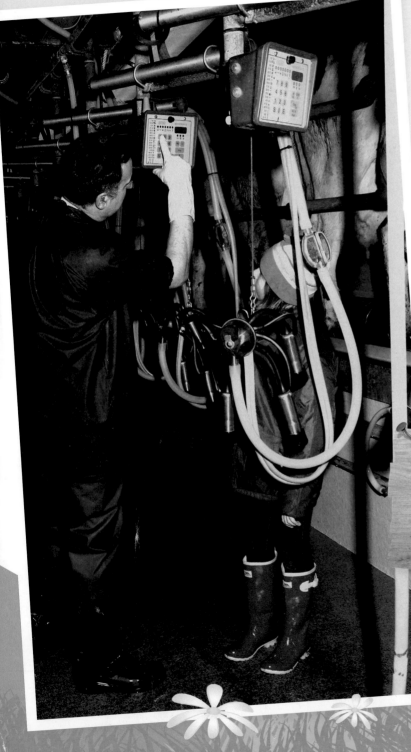

Peter has more computers in the milking parlour. These computers keep a record of how much milk each cow produces. They also work out how much 'cow cake' each cow needs.

Emily watches Peter put the information into the computer.

Time to go home

After milking, the equipment is cleaned again. Now the cows are ready to go back to their stalls for the night. Emily and Peter close all the doors and go back to the farmhouse.

Emily helps Peter herd the cows back to their stalls.

The cows aren't the only ones who are ready for bed. Emily is tired! It has been a long, hard day.

EMILY'S DIARY

That was the best day ever! The cows are so friendly and calm and I don't mind the smell any more. But now I can't keep my eyes open!

Peter thanks Emily for helping him with the cows.

Glossary

Cow cake a special mixture of food made from the remains of pressing oilseeds. It is rich in vitamins and minerals

Digest to break down and absorb food in the stomach

Equipment the tools and machines the farmer uses to do his job

Injection medicine, which is given by putting a needle through the skin

Maize a cereal crop grown by the farmer. It is also called corn

Manure the smelly waste produced by a cow

Milking parlour the special room where all the cows are milked

Silage a nutrient-rich mixture of soya, grain and fermented grass. Silage is often used as part of the cows' diet during winter

Udders the large pink bag-like part of the cow, where the milk comes from

Index

Helping Out

Contents of titles in the series:

FARM

An early start
Cleaning the cow barn
Milking time
Feeding the calves
Cleaning the equipment
Feeding the cows
Chewing the cud
A visit from the vet
More milking
Time to go home

AQUARIUM

Visiting the aquarium
Looking in the tanks
Food preparation
Feeding the rays
Water samples
The rainforest area
Feeding the sharks
Coral reef zone
Feeding the turtles
Time to go home

ZOO

Meeting the keepers
Looking around
Important jobs
Preparing the food
Meeting the lemurs
Feeding the lemurs
Cleaning and sweeping
Lemur play
Lemur babies
A brilliant day

DOG RESCUE CENTRE

Saying hello
Meeting the dogs
A new arrival
Cleaning the kennels
Time for a walk
Feeding the puppies
A visit to the vet
Training fun
Finding a home
Time to say goodbye

WAYLAND